WELCOME TO MY CABIN

NANCY SMITH & LYNDA MILLIGAN

CREDITS

Sharon Holmes – Editor, Technical Illustrator
Susie Johnson – Cover Design, Photo Stylist, Quilt Design
Lexie Foster – Illustration, Photo Stylist, Quilt Design
Christine Scott – Editorial Assistant
Sandi Fruehling – Copy Reader
Brad Bartholomew – Photographer

THANKS

Sewing & Machine Quilting – Ann Petersen, Jane Dumler, Katie Wells,
Susan Auskaps, Sue Williams, Courtenay Hughes
Long-arm Machine Quilting – Sandi Fruehling, Carolyn Schmitt
On-site Photography - Crate and Barrel Furniture

Special thanks to Barbara Karst for her suggestions and her hard work
in making the original Saturday Sampler quilt that inspired this book.

POSSIBILITIES®

...Fabric designers for AvLyn, Inc., publishers of DreamSpinners®
patterns & I'll Teach Myself™ & Possibilities® books...

Home of Great American Quilt Factory, Inc.

WELCOME TO MY CABIN

Published in the United States of America by Possibilities®, Denver, Colorado
ISBN: 1-880972-50-6

CABIN IN THE WOODS

Living in Colorado makes us aware of the beauty of nature—the crystal blue skies—the purple mountains' majesty. We designed this quilt for a Saturday Sampler class in our retail store, and the reception was so great that we decided to publish the pattern for others to enjoy.

Being aware of quilters' different skill levels, as well as time frames and space limitations, we decided to extract several of the elements from the main quilt and present other quilt options. A leaf quilt may be just perfect for symbolizing a New England fall. An eagle wall hanging or pillow may be just the outdoorsy note needed for the family room. Whichever option you choose from the 14 possibilities, we hope you will enjoy feelings of warmth and coziness from your efforts.

Cabin in the Woods can be made from your fabric stash, or use the detailed yardage chart on page 3. Pages 4 through 8 contain complete cutting charts for the quilt, fabric by fabric.

CABIN IN THE WOODS - YARDAGE

62 x 62″

Use fabric with 42″ usable width.

TIPS: Use photo as a guide when selecting fabrics. Use diagram below and cutting charts on pages 4-8 as aids in identification of quilt elements and fabrics. Label all fabrics as they are purchased.

Directions are for fusible web applique—purchase 5 yards.

YARDAGE

● Light Brown	¼ yd	cabin block, earth unit, tree trunks, spring acorns
● Medium brown #1	⅝ yd	cabin block, earth unit, Border 3
● Medium brown #2	⅓ yd	cabin block, earth unit, leaf block, leaf block stems, Border 2
● Dark browns	⅙ yd ea of 2	earth unit, fall acorns
● Black-brown	⅓ yd	bear, fish eyes
● Tans	⅜ yd ea of 3	leaf block background; Border 3; canoe; fall acorns; both deer; fish fins, tails, & eyes; spring acorns; spring vine
● Oranges	⅙ yd ea of 3	leaf blocks, fall leaves, cabin door, fish underside
● Rusts	⅙ yd ea of 2	cabin roof, fall leaves
● Navy #1	⅓ yd	Border 1, Flying Geese & mountain units
● Navy #2	1⅔ yd	Border 5 (cut on lengthwise grain)
● Medium & dark blues	¼ yd ea of 5	sky of tree blocks, Flying Geese & mountain units, Border 2, corner blocks, leaf block
● Light blues #1, 4, 6	¼ yd ea of 3	sky of mountain & cabin blocks, columbines
● Light blues #2, 3, 5	⅙ yd ea of 3	sky of mountain & tree blocks
● Bright blue #1	⅛ yd	Border 2
● Bright blue #2	⅙ yd	Border 3
● Med & dark purples	⅓ yd ea of 6	mountain unit, corner blocks, Border 4, leaf block, horizontal sashing between leaf blocks
● Light purple	⅙ yd	vertical sashing to left of leaf blocks, bear tracks
● Lavender	⅛ yd	columbine tails
● Dark blue-greens	⅜ yd ea of 2	Flying Geese & mountain units, corner blocks, cabin under-roof, horizontal sashing near earth and Flying Geese unit
● Light & med blue-greens	⅓ yd ea of 3	sky of tree blocks, water
● Dark greens	⅓ yd ea of 2	tree row 4 (bottom), Flying Geese unit
● Med-dark green	½ yd	tree row 3, columbine vine, cabin grass, spring leaves, columbine leaves, canoe trim
● Med-light green	½ yd	tree row 2, fall vine, cabin grass, spring leaves, columbine leaves
● Light greens	⅙ yd ea of 2	tree row 1 (top), spring leaves
● Yellow-green	⅛ yd	fish upper side
● Yellow #1	⅛ yd	columbine centers, eagle beak
● Yellow #2	⅛ yd	cabin windows, fall leaves
● Golds	⅙ yd ea of 2	leaf block, fall leaves, canoe
● Dark gray	⅛ yd	chimney, eagle
● Light gray	⅛ yd	eagle
White	⅛ yd	eagle, columbines
Binding	⅝ yd	
Backing	4⅛ yd	
Batting	68 x 68″	

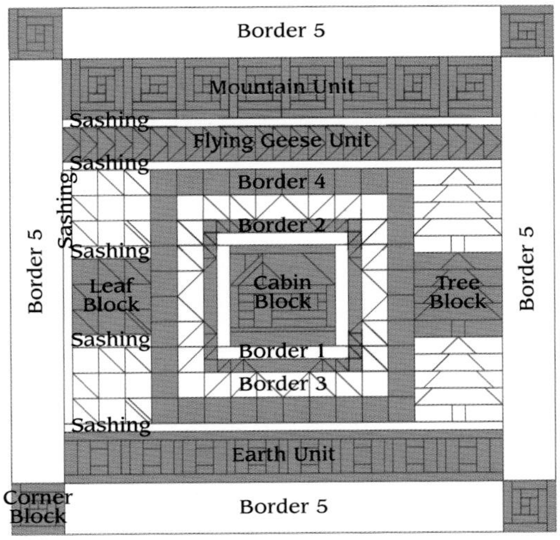

Diagram labels: Border 5, Mountain Unit, Sashing, Flying Geese Unit, Border 4, Border 2, Leaf Block, Cabin Block, Tree Block, Border 1, Border 3, Earth Unit, Corner Block, Border 5

CABIN IN THE WOODS - CUTTING

When strips appear in cutting list, cut crossgrain strips (selvage to selvage) unless otherwise noted.
Tape fabric swatches on the rectangles below.

Patterns, pages 42-48, are given for fusible web applique, reversed and ready to be traced. Reverse patterns and add seam allowance if doing hand applique.

CUTTING *Cut these squares in HALF diagonally

PLACE FABRIC SWATCHES HERE

● Light brown	cabin block	1 strip 1½" wide
	earth unit	1 strip 1½" wide
	tree trunks	3 pieces 2½ x 2"
	spring acorn tops	See page 17
● Med brown #1	cabin block	1 strip 1½" wide
	earth unit	1 strip 2" wide
		3 strips 1½" wide
	Border 3	*8 squares 3⅞"
		8 squares 3½"
● Med brown #2	cabin block	1 strip 1½" wide
	earth unit	1 strip 2" wide
	leaf block	3 squares 3½"
	leaf block stems	3 pieces 1 x 6"
	Border 2	4 squares 2"
		*8 squares 2⅜"
● Dark brown #1	earth unit	1 strip 2½" wide
● Dark brown #2	earth unit	1 strip 1½" wide
	fall acorn tops	See page 17
● Black-brown	bear	See page 19
	fish eyes (centers)	See page 18

● Tan #1	leaf block background	*1 square 4"
		*2 squares 3⅞"
		1 square 3½"
	Border 3	4 squares 3½"
		*8 squares 3⅞"
	canoe top	See page 18
	fall acorn bottoms	See page 17
● Tan #2	leaf block background	*1 square 4"
		*2 squares 3⅞"
		1 square 3½"
	deer - female	See page 19
	fish fins, tails, eyes	See page 18
	spring acorn bottoms	See page 17
● Tan #3	spring vine	1½ strips 3¼" wide
	deer - male	See page 19

CABIN IN THE WOODS - CUTTING

● Orange #1	leaf block	*2 squares 3⅞″	
	fall leaves	See page 17	
● Orange #2	leaf block	*2 squares 3⅞″	
	cabin door	1 piece 2½ x 4½″ (U)	
	fish underside	See page 18	
● Orange #3	leaf block	3 squares 3½″	
● Rust #1	cabin roof	1 piece 4¼ x 8¾″ (I)	
		1 square 4¼″ (H)	
● Rust #2	fall leaves	See page 17	

● Navy #1	Border 1	2 strips 2″ wide	
	mountain unit	1 strip 1½″ wide	
	Flying Geese unit	1 strip 2½″ wide	
● Navy #2	Border 5	4 strips 6½″ x length of fabric (cut on lengthwise grain)	
● Med or dk blue #1	sky of tree blocks (row 3)	1 strip 2½″ wide	
● Med or dk blue #2	sky of tree blocks (row 5)	1 strip 2½″ wide	
	Flying Geese unit	1 strip 2½″ wide	
● Med or dk blue #3	mountain unit, corner blocks	3 strips 1½″ wide	
	Flying Geese unit	1 strip 2½″ wide	
● Med or dk blue #4	mountain unit	1 strip 1½″ wide	
	Border 2	*8 squares 2⅜″	
		8 squares 2″	
● Med or dk blue #5	mountain unit, corner blocks	1 strip 1½″ wide	
	leaf block	*2 squares 3⅞″	

CABIN IN THE WOODS - CUTTING

PLACE FABRIC
SWATCHES HERE

● Light blue #1	sky of mountain unit	3 strips 1½″ wide
● Light blue #2	sky of mountain unit	2 strips 1½″ wide
● Light blue #3	sky of mountain unit	1 strip 1½″ wide
● Light blue #4	sky of cabin block	1 piece 1½ x 12½″ (A)
		1 square 4¼″ (B)
		2 pieces 1½ x 5½″ (C)
		1 piece 2¼ x 5″ (D)
		1 piece 1 x 5″ (E)
● Light blue #5	sky of tree blocks (row 1)	1 strip 2½″ wide
● Light blue #6	columbines	See page 18

● Bright blue #1	Border 2	4 pieces 2 x 9½″
● Bright blue #2	Border 3	4 pieces 3½ x 6½″

● Med or dk purple #1	mountain unit, corner blocks	3 strips 1½″ wide
	Border 4	6 squares 3½″
● Med or dk purple #2	corner blocks	1 strip 1½″ wide
	Border 4	6 squares 3½″
● Med or dk purple #3	Border 4	6 squares 3½″
● Med or dk purple #4	Border 4	6 squares 3½″
● Med or dk purple #5	Border 4	6 squares 3½″
	leaf block	3 squares 3½″
● Med or dk purple #6	horiz sashing of leaf blocks	1 strip 2″ wide
	Border 4	6 squares 3½″
● Light purple	vertical sashing	1 strip 1½″ wide
	bear tracks	See page 11
● Lavender	columbine tails	See page 18

CABIN IN THE WOODS - CUTTING

● Dk blue-green #1	Flying Geese unit	1 strip 2½″ wide
	mountain unit	1 strip 1½″ wide
	corner blocks	1 strip 1½″ wide
	cabin under-roof	2 squares 3¼″ (J)
● Dk blue-green #2	Flying Geese unit	1 strip 2½″ wide
	corner blocks	1 strip 1½″ wide
	horizontal sashing	4 strips 1½″ wide
● Lt or med blue-green #1	sky of tree blocks (row 4)	1 strip 2½″ wide
	water (top)	2 strips 3″ wide
● Lt or med blue-green #2	sky of tree blocks (row 2)	1 strip 2½″ wide
	water (middle)	2 strips 3¼″ wide
● Lt or med blue-green #3	water (bottom)	2 strips 4″ wide

● Dark green #1	tree row 4	1 strip 2½″ wide
	Flying Geese unit	1 strip 2½″ wide
● Dark green #2	Flying Geese unit	1 strip 2½″ wide
● Med-dark green	tree row 3	1 strip 2½″ wide
	columbine vine	1½ strips 3¼″ wide
	cabin grass	2¼ x 12½″ (G)
	spring leaves	See page 17
	columbine leaves	See page 18
	canoe trim	See page 18
● Med-light green	tree row 2	1 strip 2½″ wide
	fall vine	1½ strips 3¼″ wide
	cabin grass	1 x 12½″ (F)
	spring leaves	See page 17
	columbine leaves	See page 18
● Light green #1	tree row 1	1 strip 2½″ wide
	spring leaves	See page 17
● Light green #2	spring leaves	See page 17
● Yellow-green	fish upper side	See page 18

CABIN IN THE WOODS - CUTTING

PLACE FABRIC
SWATCHES HERE

Yellow #1	columbine centers	See page 18
	eagle beak	See page 16
Yellow #2	cabin windows	2 pieces 1½ x 2½″ (V)
	fall leaves	See page 17
Gold #1	leaf block	*1 square 4″
		*2 squares 3⅞″
		1 square 3½″
	fall leaves	See page 17
Gold #2	canoe bottom	See page 18

Dark gray	chimney	1 piece 2 x 5″ (W)
	eagle top layer	See page 16
Light gray	eagle bottom layer	See page 16
White	eagle head	See page 16
	columbines	See page 18

Binding   7 strips 2½″ wide

CABIN IN THE WOODS - CABIN BLOCK

IMPORTANT NOTE: Due to the medallion style of this quilt, each element must be pieced accurately for the successive parts to fit. Therefore, exact cut sizes are given for all pieces of the quilt, including the long sashing strips and the borders. At the beginning of the directions for each element, the finished size, not including seam allowance, is given.

DIRECTIONS

Size - 12 x 12"

1. ADDITIONAL CUTTING:

   a. From 1½" light brown strip:
      N   2 pieces 2¼" long
      O   1 piece 2¾" long
      P   1 piece 6¾" long
      Q   2 pieces 1½" long

   b. From 1½" medium brown #1 strip:
      K   1 piece 10½" long
      L   1 piece 2¼" long
      M   1 piece 6¾" long

   c. From 1½" medium brown #2 strip:
      R   1 piece 2¼" long
      S   1 piece 2¾" long
      T   2 pieces 1½" long

2. CHIMNEY UNIT: Stitch pieces D, W, and E right sides together following diagram. Press. Trim top and bottom edges to make a 4¼" square. Stitch J to H, right sides together, as shown. Trim, leaving ¼" seam allowance. Press. Place DWE unit and HJ units right sides together as shown. Mark from corner to corner as shown. Stitch and trim. Press.

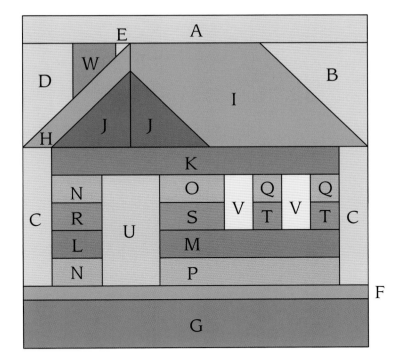

3. ROOF UNIT: Stitch J and B to I right sides together as shown. Trim, and press.

4. SIDING UNIT: Stitch pieces right sides together following diagrams. Stitch sky pieces, C, to each side. Press.

5. ASSEMBLE BLOCK: Stitch parts of block together in rows, adding sky, A, at top of block and grass, F and G, at bottom. Press.

2. CHIMNEY UNIT

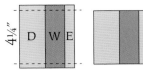

Trim to 4¼"   Stitch   Trim

Stitch on mark & trim

Mark or crease from corner to corner   Open out & press

3. ROOF UNIT

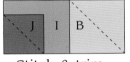

Stitch & trim

4. SIDING UNIT

5. Assemble in rows

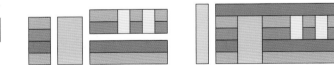

DIRECTIONS

Size after Border 1 - 15″

Size after Border 2 - 18″

1. ADDITIONAL CUTTING from navy #1 strips:
   2 pieces 12½″ long
   2 pieces 15½″ long

2. BORDER 1: Stitch short navy pieces to sides of block. Stitch long navy pieces to top and bottom. Press.

3. BORDER 2:

   a. Make 16 half-square triangle units with triangles cut from medium brown #2 and medium or dark blue #4 squares. Press.

   b. Make 4 side units as shown using bright blue #1 rectangles and medium or dark blue #4 squares. Press.

   c. Make 2 side borders from units in Steps a and b. Make top and bottom borders from units in Steps a and b and medium brown #2 squares. Press.

   d. Stitch side borders to block. Stitch top and bottom borders to block. Press.

2.

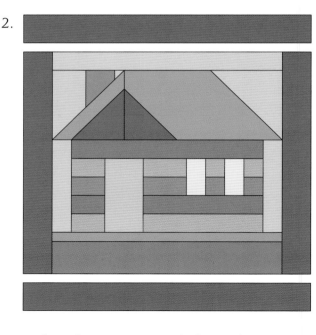

Make 16

3a.

Stitch & Trim

3b.

Open & Press

Make 4

Make 2 - Side Borders

3c.

Make 2 - Top & Bottom Borders

3d.

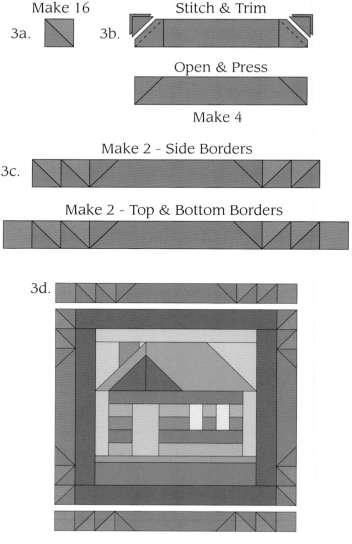

CABIN IN THE WOODS - BORDERS 3 & 4

DIRECTIONS

Size after Border 3 - 24″

Size after Border 4 - 30″

Applique patterns are given for fusible web applique, reversed and ready to be traced.

1. BORDER 3:

   a. Make 16 half-square triangle units using triangles cut from tan #1 and medium brown #1. Press.

   b. FLYING GEESE UNITS: Make 4 units as shown using bright blue #2 rectangles and medium brown #1 squares. Press.

   c. Make 2 side borders from units made in Steps 1 and 2. Make top and bottom borders from units made in Steps 1-2, and tan #1 squares. Press.

   d. Stitch side borders to quilt as shown. Stitch top and bottom borders to quilt as shown. Press.

2. BORDER 4:

   a. Mixing medium and dark purple squares as desired, stitch 8 together for each side border and 10 together for top and bottom borders. Press. See diagram.

   b. Stitch side borders to quilt. Stitch top and bottom borders to quilt. Press.

   c. Trace 6 bear tracks to fusible web. Trace 6 reversed. Applique 5 light purple bear tracks to left end of bottom border, alternating "left" and "right" tracks and angling each slightly. Applique 4 to right end of top border and 3 to top end of right border, alternating and angling as before. See diagram.

1a. 1b.

Make 16   Stitch & Trim   Repeat   Make 4

1c.   Make 2 Sides

Make 2 Top & Bottom

1d.

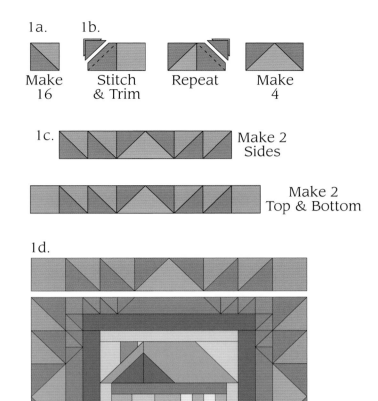

2b-c.

2a.

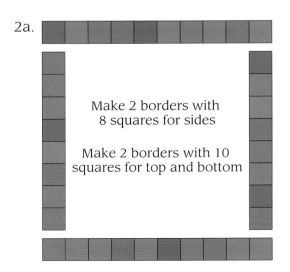

Make 2 borders with 8 squares for sides

Make 2 borders with 10 squares for top and bottom

CABIN IN THE WOODS - LEAF BLOCKS

DIRECTIONS

Size of leaf block - 9″

Size of leaf block unit with sashing - 10x30″

1. TOP BLOCK:
    a. Make 4 half-square triangle units using triangles cut from tan #1 and orange #2 squares (3⅞″ squares). Press.
    b. Using paper piecing pattern on page 42, make 1 stem unit with triangles cut from tan #1 square (4″ square) and medium brown #2 rectangle (1x6″). Press.
    c. Arrange units and orange #3 squares as shown. Stitch into 3 rows. Stitch rows together. Press.

2. MIDDLE BLOCK:
    a. Make 4 half-square triangle units using triangles cut from gold #1 and orange #1 squares (3⅞″ squares). Press.
    b. Using paper piecing pattern on page 42, make 1 stem unit with triangles cut from gold #1 square (4″ square) and medium brown #2 rectangle (1x6″). Press.
    c. Arrange units and medium brown #2 squares as shown. Stitch into 3 rows. Stitch rows together. Press.

3. BOTTOM BLOCK:
    a. Make 4 half-square triangle units using triangles cut from tan #2 and medium or dark blue #5 squares (3⅞″ squares). Press.
    b. Using paper piecing pattern on page 42, make 1 stem unit with triangles cut from tan #2 square (4″ square) and medium brown #2 rectangle (1x6″). Press.
    c. Arrange units and medium or dark purple #5 squares as shown. Stitch into 3 rows. Stitch rows together. Press.

4. HORIZONTAL SASHING: Cut 2 segments from 2″ strip of medium or dark purple #6, each 9½″ long. Stitch blocks and sashing together as shown. Press.

5. VERTICAL SASHING: Cut one piece of sashing 30½″ long from 1½″ wide strip of light purple. Stitch to left side of leaf block row. Press.

 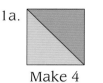

1a. Make 4   1b. Make 1

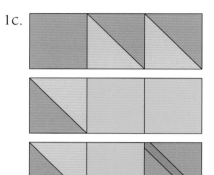

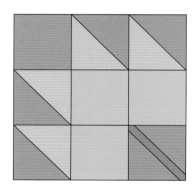

4.

5.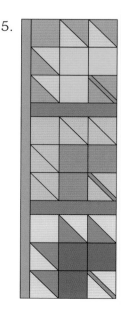

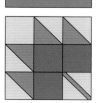

CABIN IN THE WOODS - TREE BLOCKS

DIRECTIONS

Size of tree block - 10″

Size of tree block unit - 10x30″

1. ADDITIONAL CUTTING: Use chart at right to subcut pieces A-I from the designated 2½″ strips.

2. ROW 1: Place A on B right sides together as shown. Mark a diagonal line. Stitch on line. Trim, leaving ¼″ seam allowance. Press. Repeat on opposite end.

3. ROW 2: Repeat Step 2 using C and D.

4. ROW 3: Repeat Step 2 using E and F.

5. ROW 4: Repeat Step 2 using G and H.

6. ROW 5: Using I and J (light brown 2½ x 2″), make unit as shown. Press.

7. ASSEMBLE: Arrange rows in order and stitch. Press. Make 3.

8. ROW: Stitch the 3 blocks into a vertical row.

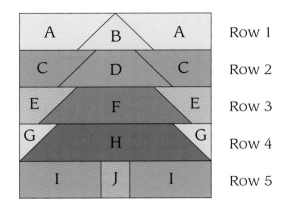

ADDITIONAL CUTTING:

A	Light blue #5	6 pieces 5½″ long
B	Light green #1	3 pieces 4½″ long
C	Light or med blue-green #2	6 pieces 4½″ long
D	Medium-light green	3 pieces 6½″ long
E	Medium or dark blue #1	6 pieces 3½″ long
F	Medium-dark green	3 pieces 8½″ long
G	Light or med blue-green #1	6 pieces 2½″ long
H	Dark green #1	3 pieces 10½″ long
I	Medium or dark blue #2	6 pieces 4¾″ long

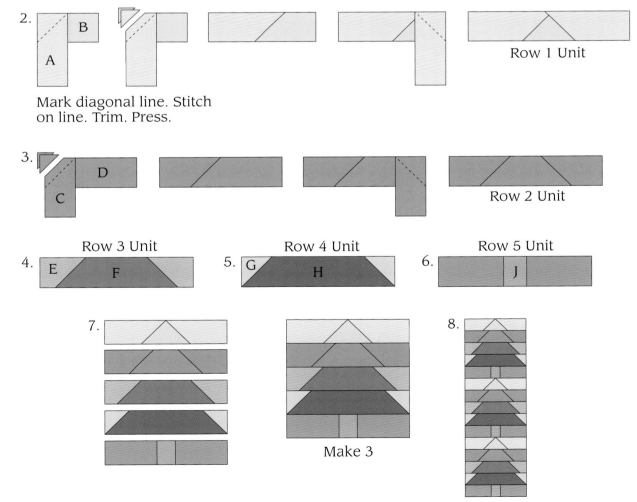

2. Mark diagonal line. Stitch on line. Trim. Press.

Row 1 Unit

3. Row 2 Unit

Row 3 Unit   Row 4 Unit   Row 5 Unit

4. E F   5. G H   6. J

7. Make 3

8.

CABIN IN THE WOODS - EARTH UNIT

DIRECTIONS

Size with top & bottom strips - 6 x 50″

1. ADDITIONAL CUTTING: Cut 2 pieces 4½″ long from 2″ medium brown #1 strip. Cut 2 pieces 4½″ long from 2″ medium brown #2 strip.

2. STRIP SET 1: Cut 1½″ dark brown #2 strip to same length as medium brown #1 and #2 strips remaining from Step 1. Make strip set as shown. Press. Crosscut into 7 units 4½″ long.

3. STRIP SET #2: Cut 1½″ light brown strip in half (21″). Cut 2½″ dark brown #1 strip to the same length. Make strip set as shown. Press. Crosscut into 8 units 2½″ long.

4. ASSEMBLE: Starting and ending with Unit 2, stitch units together alternately as shown. Press.

5. ADD END PIECES:

   a. Using pieces cut in Step 1, stitch one piece of each color together. Stitch one to each end of earth unit, keeping medium brown #1 strip to left.

   b. Stitch 1½″ medium brown #1 strips end to end. Press. Cut 2 pieces 50½″ long. Stitch one to top and one to bottom of earth unit. Press.

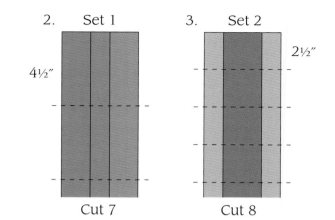

2. Set 1   3. Set 2

4½″

2½″

Cut 7   Cut 8

Unit 1   Unit 2

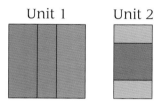

4.

5a.

5b.

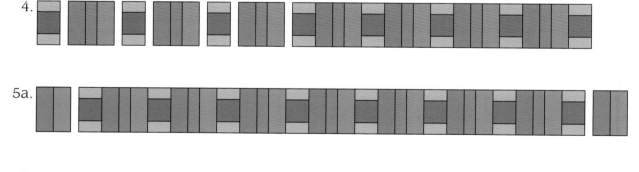

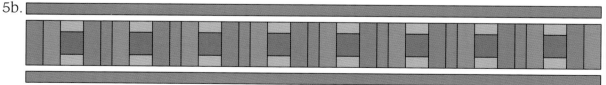

CABIN IN THE WOODS - FLYING GEESE UNIT

DIRECTIONS

Size with horizontal sashing - 6 x 50"

1. ADDITIONAL CUTTING: From each of the seven 2½" strips of blues and greens cut for Flying Geese unit, cut 4 pieces 2½ x 4½" and 8 pieces 2½ x 2½".

2. UNITS: Place a square on a rectangle, right sides together. Stitch as shown. Trim, leaving ¼" seam allowance. Press. Repeat on other end of rectangle. Mix colors as desired. Make 25.

3. ASSEMBLE: Stitch units together as shown.

4. ADD HORIZONTAL SASHING:

   a. Stitch 1½" dark blue-green #2 strips end to end (horizontal sashing). Press. Cut 3 pieces 50½" long. Stitch one to top and one to bottom of Flying Geese unit. Press.

   b. Stitch third sashing piece to top of earth unit. Size: 7 x 50".

2. Stitch   Trim   Repeat

Make 25

3.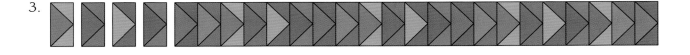

4a.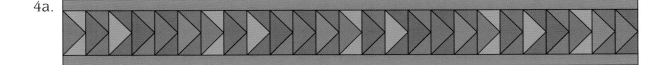

4b.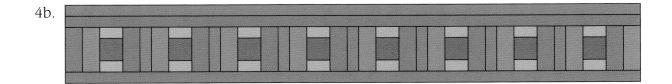

CABIN IN THE WOODS - MOUNTAIN UNIT

DIRECTIONS

Size of Block A - 7x7"

Size of Block B - 5x7"

Size of mountain unit - 7x50"

Applique patterns are given for fusible web applique, reversed and ready to be traced.

1. ADDITIONAL CUTTING from 1½" strips:

Med or dark blue #5	8 pieces 1½" long	A
Light blue #3	8 pieces 1½" long	B
	8 pieces 2½" long	C
Light blue #2	8 pieces 3½" long	D
	8 pieces 4½" long	E
Light blue #1	8 pieces 5½" long	F
	4 pieces 6½" long	G
	2 pieces 7½" long	H
Med or dark blue #3	4 pieces 2½" long	I
	4 pieces 3½" long	J
	4 pieces 4½" long	K
	4 pieces 5½" long	L
Dark blue-green #1	4 pieces 2½" long	M
	4 pieces 3½" long	N
Med or dk purple #1	4 pieces 4½" long	O
	8 pieces 5½" long	P
Navy #1	4 pieces 6½" long	Q
Med or dark blue #4	4 pieces 7½" long	R

2. BLOCKS: Working counterclockwise, make 4 of each block following diagrams. Press.

3. ASSEMBLE: Stitch blocks together alternately, as shown. Stitch piece H to each end. Press.

4. APPLIQUE: Applique eagle to second and third blocks as shown, keeping it out of top and bottom seam allowances.

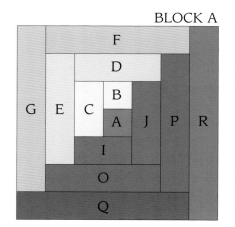

BLOCK A   BLOCK B

2. BLOCK A

Round 1

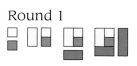

Round 2

Round 3

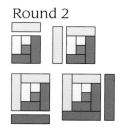

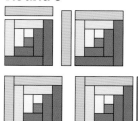

Make 4

BLOCK B

Round 1

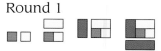

Round 2

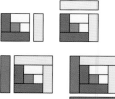

Add to top & bottom only

Make 4

3.

Add H   Add H

4.

CABIN IN THE WOODS - SPRING & FALL BORDERS

DIRECTIONS

Size - 6 x 50″

Applique patterns are given for fusible web applique, reversed and ready to be traced.

1. TRACE VINE: Cut 2 pieces of fusible web exactly 3 x 50″. Draw a line down the center of each piece—1½″ from the long sides. Trace 1 curved vine end then 7 arc-shaped vine segments in a row, end to end, as shown in diagram on page 43. Keep center line straight as you trace arcs. Finish by tracing reversed vine end segment at other end. Curved ends should face same direction. Repeat for other vine.

2. PREPARE VINE FABRIC: Stitch tan #3 strips end to end. Press seam allowance open. Repeat with medium-light green strips.

3. FUSE & CUT OUT VINE: Fuse traced vines to wrong side of seamed strips. Cut out on lines.

4. PREPARE LEAVES & ACORNS: Trace 7 oak leaves and 7 oak leaves reversed onto fusible web. Mark the reversed oak leaves "spring" and the others "fall". Trace 6 large aspen leaves. Trace 8 small aspen leaves. Trace 20 acorn bottoms and tops. Cut apart just outside lines. Fuse to wrong side of each fabric. Cut out on lines.

5. FUSE APPLIQUES ON BORDER: Cut 4 navy #2 border strips to 50½″ long. Set aside 2 for columbine and water borders. Fold each of the remaining 2 borders in half lengthwise and lightly press a center line. Open out. Peel paper backing from appliques. Arrange vines, centered both lengthwise and crosswise, on right side of borders. See diagram on page 43. Arrange leaves and acorns as shown at right. Note angle of each set of leaves and direction of curved vine ends. Keep appliques out of seam allowance. Tuck ends of aspen leaves under vines and cover stems of oak leaves with acorns. Fuse.

6. STITCH: Finish edges of appliques with machine blanket or satin stitch or use an open zigzag.

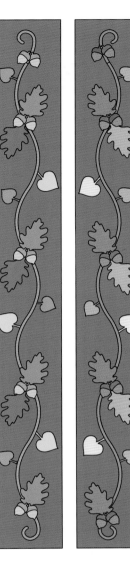

CABIN IN THE WOODS - CORNER BLOCKS

DIRECTIONS

Size - 6 x 6″

1. ADDITIONAL CUTTING from 1½″ strips:

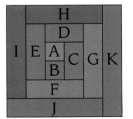

Med or dk blue #5	4 pieces 1½″ long	A
Med or dk purple #2	4 pieces 1½″ long	B
	4 pieces 2½″ long	C
Med or dk blue #3	4 pieces 2½″ long	D
	4 pieces 3½″ long	E
Dk blue-green #2	4 pieces 3½″ long	F
	4 pieces 4½″ long	G
Dk blue-green #1	4 pieces 4½″ long	H
	4 pieces 5½″ long	I
Purple #1	4 pieces 5½″ long	J
	4 pieces 6½″ long	K

2. BLOCKS: Working counterclockwise, make 4 blocks as shown. Press.

Make 4

CABIN IN THE WOODS - COLUMBINE BORDER

DIRECTIONS

Size - 6x50"

Applique patterns are given for fusible web applique, reversed and ready to be traced.

1. TRACE VINE: Refer to Step 1, Spring & Fall Borders, page 17, omitting curved vine end pieces.
2. PREPARE VINE FABRIC: Using medium-dark green strips, repeat Step 2, page 17.
3. FUSE & CUT OUT VINE: See Step 3, page 17.
4. PREPARE COLUMBINES & LEAVES: Trace 1 large columbine and 2 large columbines reversed. Trace 2 small columbines and 2 small columbines reversed. Trace 2 large leaves and 2 large leaves reversed. Trace 4 small leaves. Cut apart just outside lines. Fuse to wrong side of each fabric. Cut out on lines.
5. FUSE APPLIQUES ON BORDER: Repeat Step 5 on page 17.
6. STITCH: See Step 6, page 17.

CABIN IN THE WOODS - WATER BORDER

DIRECTIONS

Size - 6x50"

Applique patterns are given for fusible web applique, reversed and ready to be traced.

1. TRACE WATER: Cut 3 pieces of fusible web exactly 3x50½" with very straight long edges. Trace each of the 3 water pieces on page 44 five times end to end, keeping long edge of fusible web even with straight bottom edge of water patterns. Trim away excess just above curvy top edges.
2. TRACE FISH & CANOE: Trace parts for 1 fish and 1 fish reversed. Trace canoe parts, reversing at center line. Cut apart just outside lines.
3. PREPARE APPLIQUES: Stitch fabric strips for water end to end and press seam allowances open. Fuse traced water pieces to wrong sides of water fabrics. Cut out on lines. Fuse traced fish and canoe parts to appropriate fabrics and cut out on lines.
4. FUSE APPLIQUES ON BORDER: Peel paper backing from appliques. Arrange layers of water on border. Tuck canoe bottom under top edge of bottom water piece. Arrange fish as shown below. Fuse.
5. STITCH: See Step 6, page 17.

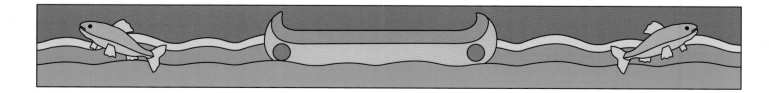

CABIN IN THE WOODS - FINISHING

Applique patterns are given for fusible web applique, reversed and ready to be traced.

1. ASSEMBLE:

   a. Stitch leaf unit and tree unit to sides of center unit. Press. Stitch water border to earth unit. Stitch earth/water to quilt. Press. Applique bear and deer. See diagram.

   b. Stitch Flying Geese unit, mountain unit, and columbine border together. Press. Stitch Geese/mountain/columbine unit to quilt. Press.

   c. Stitch corner blocks to side borders as shown. Note orientation of curved vine ends. Press. Stitch side borders to quilt. Press.

2. LAYER & QUILT: Piece backing to same size as batting. Layer, baste, and quilt.

   Optional quilting:

   a. Ditch quilt cabin block. Add detail quilting to simulate shingles, panels in door, and grass.

   b. Ditch quilt Borders 1-4. Add wavy lines in Border 1 and 4. Outline quilt bear tracks.

   c. Ditch quilt leaf and tree blocks. Add wavy lines for leaf veins and tree branches.

   d. Meander quilt earth unit. Ditch quilt water. Outline quilt bear, deer, fish, and canoe. Add curvy lines for legs on deer and bear.

   e. Ditch quilt Flying Geese unit. Quilt straight lines in mountains and curvy lines in sky above mountains.

   f. Outline quilt eagle, columbines, and appliques in spring and fall borders. Ditch quilt corner blocks.

3. BIND: Stitch binding strips together end to end. Press in half lengthwise, wrong sides together. Bind quilt using ⅜″ seam allowance.

19

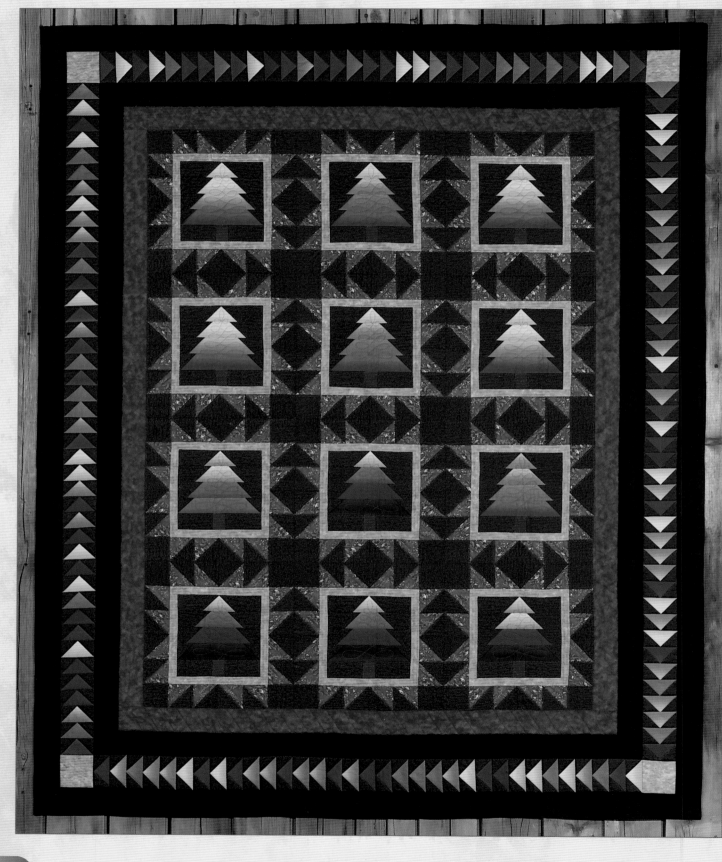

80x98″ 10″ block

Use fabric with 42″ usable width.

When strips appear in cutting list, cut crossgrain strips (selvage to selvage).

YARDAGE

Navy	block background, sashing, Border 3	4⅓ yd
Greens	trees, Border 3	
	light	⅔ yd
	medium-light	⅔ yd
	medium-dark	¾ yd
	dark	⅞ yd
Brown	trunks	⅛ yd
Gold	frames, corners	1 yd
Red #1	sashing	1⅓ yd
Red #2	Border 1	⅞ yd
Black	Borders 2, 4	2 yd
Binding		⅞ yd
Backing		7⅝ yd
Batting		86x104″

CUTTING *Cut these squares in HALF diagonally

Navy	block bkg Row 1	24 pieces 2½ x 5½″
	block bkg Row 2	24 pieces 2½ x 4½″
	block bkg Row 3	24 pieces 2½ x 3½″
	block bkg Row 4	24 pieces 2½ x 2½″
	block bkg Row 5	24 pieces 2½ x 4¾″
	sashing	48 squares 3½″
		*96 squares 3⅞″
	Border 3	300 squares 2½″
Greens	light	12 pieces 2½ x 4½″
	medium-light	12 pieces 2½ x 6½″
	medium-dark	12 pieces 2½ x 8½″
	dark	12 pieces 2½ x 10½″
	all 4 shades	38 pieces 2½ x 4½″ each
Brown		12 pieces 2½ x 2″
Gold	frames	24 pieces 1½ x 10½″
	frames	24 pieces 1½ x 12½″
	corners	4 squares 4½″
Red #1		*96 squares 3⅞″
Red #2		7 strips 3½″ wide
Black		16-17 strips 3½″ wide
Binding		10 strips 2½″ wide

1. FOR ONE BLOCK:

Mark diagonal line. Stitch on line. Trim. Press. Repeat.

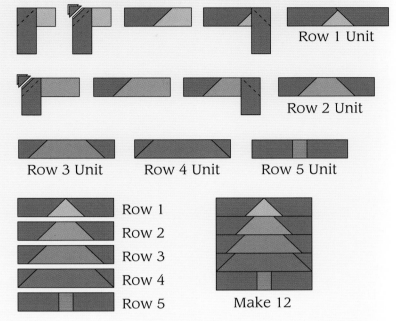

Row 1 Unit
Row 2 Unit
Row 3 Unit   Row 4 Unit   Row 5 Unit
Row 1
Row 2
Row 3
Row 4
Row 5
Make 12

DIRECTIONS

Use ¼″ seam allowance unless otherwise noted.

1. BLOCKS: Use light green for Row 1, medium-light for Row 2, medium-dark for Row 3, and dark green for Row 4. Make 12 blocks following diagrams. Press.

2. FRAMES: Stitch short pieces to sides of blocks. Stitch long pieces to top and bottom. Press. Remaining diagrams are on page 22.

3. SASHING: Make sashing units for each block as shown. Stitch short pieces to sides of blocks. Stitch long pieces to top and bottom. Press.

4. ROWS: Stitch blocks into 4 rows of 3. Stitch rows together. Press.

5. BORDERS 1 & 2: Measure length of quilt. Piece Border 1 strips to this measurement and stitch to sides of quilt. Measure width of quilt. Piece Border 1 strips to this measurement for top and bottom of quilt. Stitch to quilt. Press. Repeat for Border 2.

Continued on page 22.

Into the Forest

Continued from page 21.

6. BORDER 3: Make 150 Flying Geese units following Step 2 diagrams on page 15. Stitch units into 2 side borders of 42 units each. Stitch units into 2 top and bottom borders of 33 units each. Stitch corner squares to each end of top and bottom borders. Stitch side borders to quilt. Stitch top and bottom borders to quilt. Press.

7. BORDER 4: Repeat Step 5.

8. LAYER, QUILT, & BIND: Piece backing horizontally to same size as batting. Layer, baste, and quilt as desired. Trim backing and batting even with top. Stitch binding strips together end to end. Press in half lengthwise, wrong sides together. Bind quilt using ⅜″ seam allowance.

2.

3.

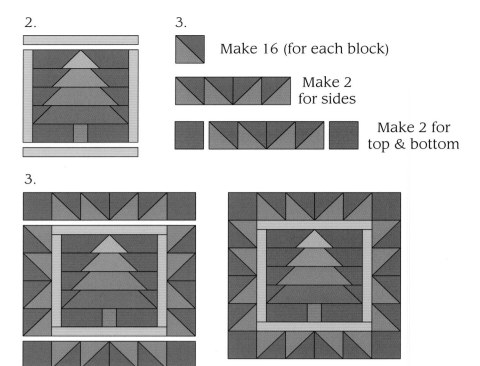

Make 16 (for each block)

Make 2 for sides

Make 2 for top & bottom

3.

4.

7.

6.

Border 3 - Sides - Make 2

Border 3 - Top & bottom - Make 2

WREATH & CABIN WALL HANGINGS

26x26"

Use fabric with 42" usable width.

When strips appear in cutting list, cut crossgrain strips (selvage to selvage).

Patterns are given for fusible web applique, reversed and ready to be traced. Be sure to have plenty of fusible web on hand if using this method. Reverse patterns and add seam allowance if doing hand applique.

YARDAGE

WREATH

Navy	background	⅝ yd
Browns	Border 1	⅙ yd
	applique, Border 2	⅛ yd ea of 2
Rusts	applique, Border 2	¼ yd ea of 3
Blues	Border 2	¼ yd ea of 4
Gold, tan, lt brown, dark brown	applique	⅛ yd each

CABIN

Tans	cabin, Border 3	¼ yd ea of 4
Browns	cabin, Border 3	⅙ yd ea of 5
Red	cabin, Bdrs 1 & 3	¼ yd
Multicolor print	Border 2	¼ yd
Blue	sky	¼ yd
Green	grass	⅛ yd ea of 2
Black	roof	⅙ yd
Yellow	windows	⅛ yd
Binding (for 1 quilt)		⅓ yd
Backing (for 1 quilt)		⅞ yd
Batting (for 1 quilt)		30x30"

CUTTING

WREATH - Patterns on page 43

Navy	background	1 square 16½"
Browns	Border 1	2 pieces 1½x16½" 2 pieces 1½x18½"
	Border 2	12 squares 2½" of each
	appliques	see Step 1
Rusts	Border 2	4 squares 4½" of 1 fabric 4 pieces 2½x4½" of each
	appliques	see Step 1
Blues	Border 2	6 pieces 2½x4½" of each 12 squares 2½" of each
Gold, tan, lt brn, dk brn		see Step 1

CABIN

Tans	cabin "logs"	1 strip 1½" wide of 3 fabrics
	Border 3	18 squares 2½" of each
Browns	cabin	2 squares 3¼" of 1 fabric (J)
	Border 3	9 pieces 2½x4½" of 4 fabrics
Red	cabin	1 piece 2x5" (W) 1 piece 2½x4½" (U)
	Border 1	2 pieces 1½x12½" 2 pieces 1½x14½"
	Border 3	4 squares 4½"
Multi	Border 2	2 pieces 2½x14½" 2 pieces 2½x18½"
Blue	sky	1 piece 1½x12½" (A) 1 square 4¼" (B) 2 pieces 1½x5½" (C) 1 piece 2¼x5" (D) 1 piece 1x5" (E)
Green	grass	1 piece 1x12½" (F) 1 piece 2¼x12½" (G)
Black	roof	1 square 4¼" (H) 1 piece 4¼x8¾" (I)
Yellow	windows	2 pieces 1½x2½" (V)
Binding (for 1 quilt)		3 strips 2¼" wide

Continued on page 41.

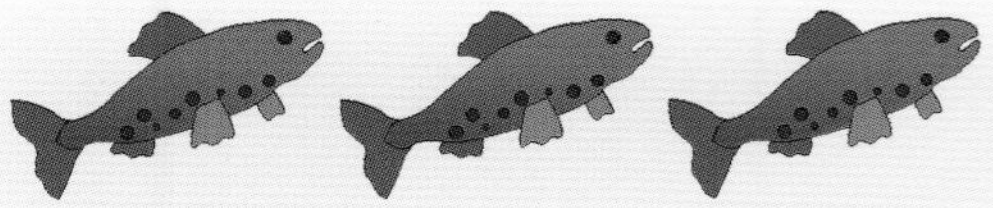

61x55″

Use fabric with 42″ usable width.

When strips appear in cutting list, cut crossgrain strips (selvage to selvage).

Patterns, page 45, are given for fusible web applique, reversed and ready to be traced. Be sure to have plenty of fusible web on hand if using this method. Reverse patterns and add seam allowance if doing hand applique.

YARDAGE

Greens		¼ yd each of 14
Light blue	sky of tree, cabin, & canoe rows	1 yd
Medium blues	sky of tree rows	¼ yd each of 3
	water of fish row, sashing	½ yd
Dark blue	sky of tree rows, sashing	⅜ yd
Lt, med, & dk blue-green	water of canoe row	⅓ yd each
Med browns	cabins	⅛ yd each of 5
Dark browns	cabins, leaf blocks	⅙ yd each of 5
	tree trunks, Bdr 1, fish eyes	½ yd
Tan	fish fins & tails	⅛ yd
Rusts	chimneys, doors, leaf blocks	⅛ yd each of 2
Golds	windows, canoe	⅙ yd each of 3
Yellow-green	fish upper side	⅛ yd
Tan-green	fish underside	⅛ yd
Binding		⅝ yd
Backing		3¾ yd
Batting		67x61″

CUTTING *Cut in HALF diagonally

Greens	roofs	4 pieces 4¼x8¾″ (I)
		4 squares 4¼″ (H)
	canoe accents	2
	trees	1 strip 2½″ wide - 8 fabrics
	Border 2	9 pieces 2½x5″ - 12 fabrics
	leaf stem unit	*4 squares 3″ - 1 fabric
	leaf bkg	*8 squares 2⅜″ - 1 fabric
		4 squares 2″ - 1 fabric

Continued on page 26.

1.

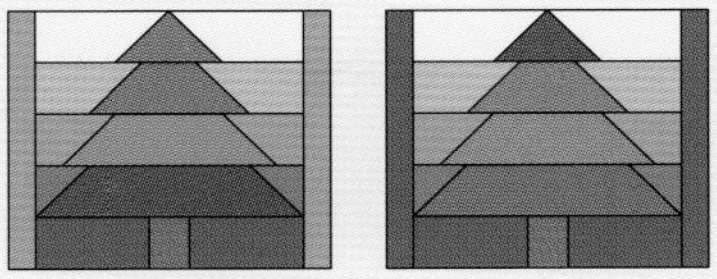

Make 4 Make 4

1.

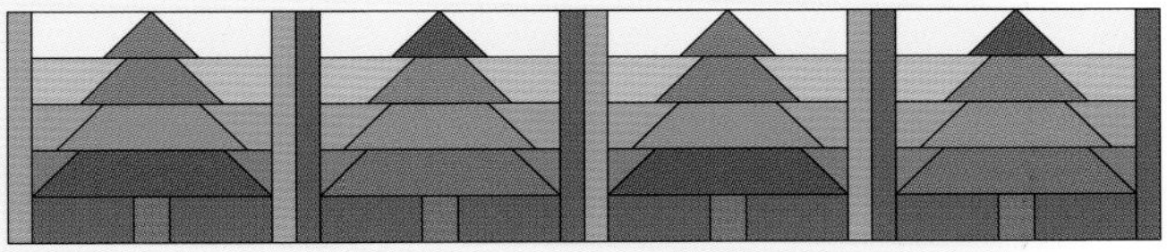

2. 3.

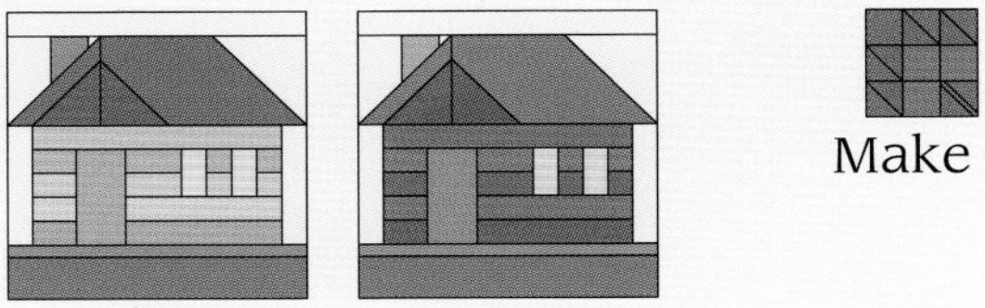

Make 2 Make 2 Make 4

2.

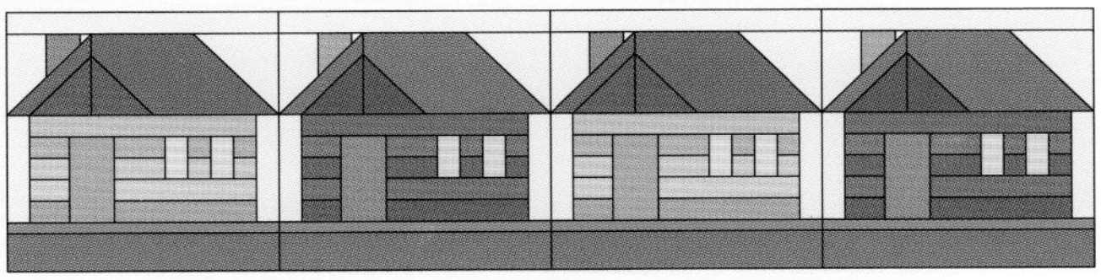

4.

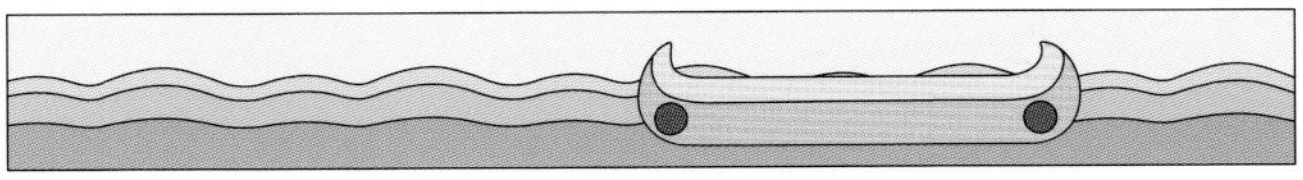

5.

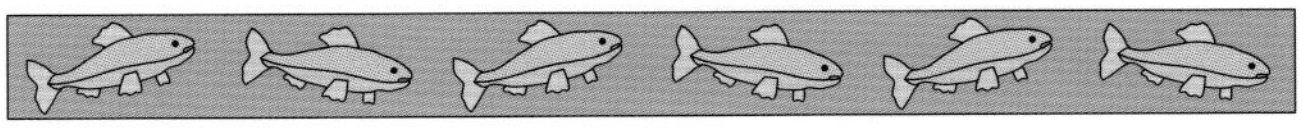

6.

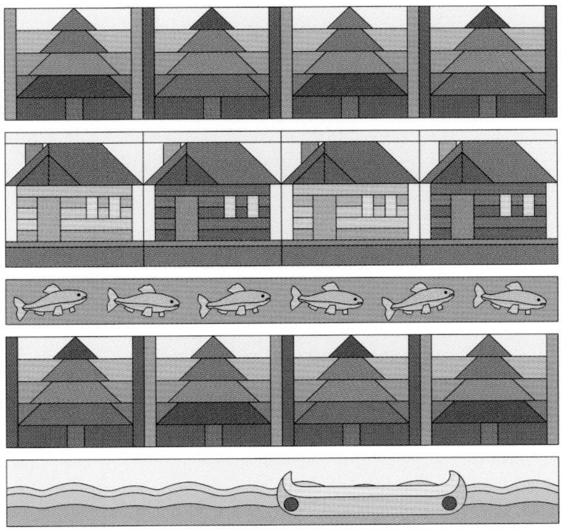

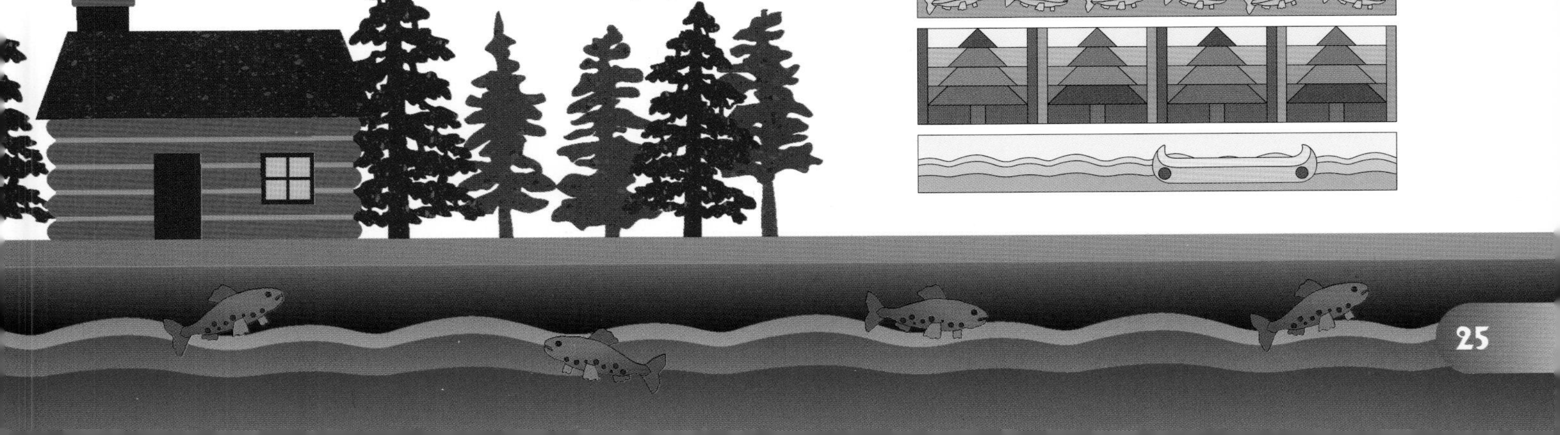

Lakefront Property

Continued from page 25.

	grass	4 pieces 1 x 12½" (F)
		4 pieces 2¼ x 12½" (G)
Light blue	sky - trees	3 strips 2½" wide
	sky - cabins	4 pieces 1½ x 12½" (A)
		4 squares 4¼" (B)
		8 pieces 1½ x 5½" (C)
		4 pieces 2¼ x 5" (D)
		4 pieces 1 x 5" (E)
	sky - canoe row	2 strips 6½" wide
Med blues	sky - trees	2 strips 2½" wide - 3 fabrics
	water - fish row	2 strips 4½" wide
	sashing	8 pieces 1½ x 10½"
Dark blue	sky - trees	2 strips 2½" wide
	sashing	8 pieces 1½ x 10½"
Blue-greens	water -	
	canoe row	2 strips 3¼" wide - 3 fabrics
Med browns	cabin "logs"	1 strip 1½" wide - 5 fabrics
Dk browns	cabin "logs"	1 strip 1½" wide - 5 fabrics
	cabin under-roof	8 squares 3¼" (J) - 2 fabrics
	leaf blocks	9 squares 2" - mixed fabrics
		*6 squares 2⅜" - mixed fabrics
	leaf stems	4 pieces 1 x 4" - mixed fabrics
	Border 1	5 strips 2½"
	tree trunks	8 pieces 2 x 2½"
	fish eyes	6
Tan	fish fins & tails	6 sets
Rusts	chimneys	4 pieces 2 x 5" (W)
	doors	4 pieces 2½ x 4½" (U)
	leaf blocks	3 squares 2"
		*2 squares 2⅜"
Golds	windows	8 pieces 1½ x 2½" (V)
	canoe	1 top, 1 bottom
Yellow-green	fish upper side	6
Tan-green	fish underside	6
Binding		6-7 strips 2¼" wide

8.

DIRECTIONS
Use ¼" seam allowance unless otherwise noted.

1. TREE BLOCKS: Make 8 tree blocks following directions in Steps 1-7 on page 13 using green fabrics in desired positions and blue fabrics in light to dark order as shown. Stitch medium blue sashing pieces to sides of 4 blocks and dark blue sashing pieces to sides of 4 blocks. Press. Stitch blocks into 2 rows of 4, alternating medium and dark sashing. Press.

2. CABIN BLOCKS: Make 2 cabins with light brown "logs" and 2 cabins with dark brown "logs". Refer to directions on page 9. Use log and roof fabrics in desired positions. Stitch blocks into a row, alternating light and dark cabins. Press.

3. LEAF BLOCKS: Make 4 small leaf blocks using Step 1 on page 12. Use fabrics in combinations desired. Paper piecing pattern for stem unit is on page 45.

4. CANOE ROW: Use directions for water border on page 18 as a guide. Stitch sky strips end to end. Press seam allowance open. Trim to 48½" long. Cut fusible web pieces 3 x 48½". Applique water layers and canoe as shown.

5. FISH ROW: Stitch water strips end to end. Press seam allowance open. Trim to 48½" long. Applique 6 fish to water as shown.

6. ASSEMBLE: Stitch rows together in order shown. Press.

7. BORDER 1: Measure length of quilt. Piece border strips to this measurement and stitch to sides of quilt. Measure width of quilt. Piece border strips to this measurement for top and bottom of quilt. Stitch to quilt. Press.

8. BORDER 2: Stitch green rectangles into 2 borders of 26 rectangles and 2 borders of 23 rectangles. There will be a few rectangles left over. Press. Stitch shorter borders to sides of quilt. Press. Stitch leaf blocks to ends of longer borders as shown. Stitch borders to top and bottom of quilt. Press.

9. LAYER, QUILT, & BIND: Piece backing vertically to same size as batting. Layer, baste, and quilt as desired. Trim backing and batting even with top. Stitch binding strips together end to end. Press in half lengthwise, wrong sides together. Bind quilt using ¼" seam allowance.

DEER, FISH, & EAGLE WALL HANGINGS

24 x 24"

Use fabric with 42" usable width.

When strips appear in cutting list, cut crossgrain strips (selvage to selvage).

Patterns, on pages 43, 44, 47, 48, are given for fusible web applique, reversed and ready to be traced. Be sure to have plenty of fusible web on hand if using this method. Reverse patterns and add seam allowance if doing hand applique.

YARDAGE

Sky		½ yd
Water, earth, clouds		⅛ yd each of 3 fabrics
Applique	deer	¼ yd
	fish	⅛ yd each of 4 fabrics
	eagles	⅛ yd each of 4 fabrics
	fish eye	scrap
Border 1		⅙ yd
Borders 2 & 3		¼ yd each of 5-6 fabrics
Binding		⅓ yd
Backing		⅞ yd
Batting		28 x 28"

CUTTING

Sky	1 square 12½"
Water, earth, clouds	see Step 1
Applique	patterns on pages 43-48
Border 1	2 pieces 2 x 12½"
	2 pieces 2 x 15½"
Borders 2 & 3	see cutting charts on pages 4-8
Binding	3 strips 2¼" wide

DIRECTIONS

Use ¼" seam allowance unless otherwise noted.

1. BLOCK: Trace 1 full segment and part of a second segment of each water (earth, cloud) piece end to end on fusible web. Pieces need to be 12½" wide. Cut apart just outside lines. Fuse to wrong sides of water (earth, cloud) fabrics. Cut out on lines. Fuse to bottom edge of sky square. Prepare remaining applique shapes. If appliqueing eagles, trace 1 set and 1 set reversed of small eagle pieces.

2. BORDER 1: Stitch shorter Border 1 pieces to sides of block. Stitch longer pieces to top and bottom. Press.

3. APPLIQUE: Applique animal(s) to block, overlapping Border 1 if desired. Press.

4. BORDERS 2 & 3: Refer to directions and diagrams on pages 10-11.

5. LAYER, QUILT, & BIND: Cut backing to same size as batting. Layer, baste, and quilt as desired. Trim backing and batting even with top. Stitch binding strips together end to end. Press in half lengthwise, wrong sides together. Bind quilt using ¼" seam allowance.

66 x 84″   9″ block

Use fabric with 42″ usable width.

When strips appear in cutting list, cut crossgrain strips (selvage to selvage).

YARDAGE

Browns	setting triangles	1 yd
	blocks	⅓ yd each of 5
Golds	setting triangles	⅜ yd each of 3
	blocks	⅓ yd each of 6
Rusts	blocks	⅓ yd each of 2
Green	blocks, Border 1	¾ yd
Purple	blocks, Border 2	1⅝ yd
Binding		⅔ yd
Backing		5⅜ yd
Batting		72 x 90″

CUTTING   *Cut in HALF diagonally

Browns	setting triangles	*12 squares 9⅞″
	blocks	**from each fabric:**
		8 squares 3½″
		*6 squares 3⅞″
		5 pieces 1 x 6″
Golds	setting triangles	**from each fabric:**
		*4 squares 9⅞″
	blocks	**from each fabric:**
		*4 squares 4″
		4 squares 3½″
		*8 squares 3⅞″
Rusts	blocks	**from each fabric:**
		8 squares 3½″
		*6 squares 3⅞″
Green	blocks	8 squares 3½″
		*6 squares 3⅞″
	Border 1	7 strips 2″ wide
Purple	blocks	8 squares 3½″
		*6 squares 3⅞″
	Border 2	8 strips 5″ wide
Binding		8 strips 2½″ wide

DIRECTIONS

Use ¼″ seam allowance unless otherwise noted.

1. BLOCKS: Mixing fabrics as desired, make 24 blocks following directions in Step 1 on page 12. There will be a few leftover pieces. Press.

2. SETTING SQUARES: Make 24 setting squares using large gold and brown triangles. Press.

3. ROWS: Arrange blocks and setting squares as shown and stitch into rows. Stitch rows together. Press.

4. BORDER 1: Measure length of quilt. Piece border strips to this measurement and stitch to sides of quilt. Measure width of quilt. Piece border strips to this measurement for top and bottom of quilt. Stitch to quilt. Press.

5. BORDER 2: Repeat Step 4.

6. LAYER, QUILT, & BIND: Piece backing vertically to same size as batting. Layer, baste, and quilt as desired. Trim backing and batting even with top. Stitch binding strips together end to end. Press in half lengthwise, wrong sides together. Bind quilt using ⅜″ seam allowance.

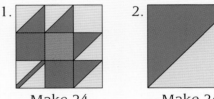

1. Make 24   2. Make 24

3.

48 x 46″   7″ and 5 x 7″ blocks

Use fabric with 42″ usable width.

When strips appear in cutting list, cut crossgrain strips (selvage to selvage).

Patterns, page 46, are given for fusible web applique, reversed and ready to be traced. Be sure to have plenty of fusible web on hand if using this method. Reverse patterns and add seam allowance if doing hand applique.

YARDAGE

Light gray-blues	Rows 1-2	⅛ yd each of 6 fabrics
Pinks	Rows 1-2	⅛ yd each of 6 fabrics
Medium blues	Row 3	⅛ yd each of 6 fabrics
Dark blues	Row 4	⅛ yd each of 6 fabrics
Purples	Row 5	⅛ yd each of 6 fabrics
Light blues	sky	⅜ yd each of 3 fabrics
White	border	1 yd
Blue-black	bear	⅓ yd
Medium blue	footprints	⅛ yd
Binding		½ yd
Backing		3¼ yd
Batting		52 x 50″

CUTTING

Fabrics for Rows 1-5	1 strip 1½″ wide of each
Fabrics for sky	8 strips 1½″ wide of each
White	5 strips 6″ wide
Appliques	1 bear; 4 footprints, 4 rev.
Binding	5 strips 2½″ wide

DIRECTIONS

Use ¼″ seam allowance unless otherwise noted.

1. BLOCKS

   a. Set aside one strip of the darkest sky fabric.

   b. Use lightest sky fabric for Round 1, medium sky fabric for Round 2, and darkest sky fabric for Round 3. Place darks (mountain fabrics) randomly, as desired.

   c. Using the stitch and trim method, add each strip to block in counterclockwise order following diagrams. Finger press seam allowance toward outside of block. Trim strip. Press blocks when all strips have been added.

   d. Make 3 Block A and 3 Block B for each row.

2. ROWS

   a. Stitch blocks alternately into rows as shown.

   b. Stitch darkest sky fabric strip to right end of each row. Trim. Press.

   c. Stitch rows together. Press.

3. BORDER: Measure length of quilt. Cut border strips to this measurement and stitch to sides of quilt. Measure width of quilt. Piece border strips to this measurement for top and bottom of quilt. Stitch to quilt. Press.

4. APPLIQUE: Applique bear and footprints to quilt using photo as a guide.

5. LAYER, QUILT, & BIND: Piece backing to same size as batting. Layer, baste, and quilt as desired. Trim backing and batting even with top. Stitch binding strips together end to end. Press in half lengthwise, wrong sides together. Bind quilt using ⅜″ seam allowance.

1c.   Stitch & Trim Method

Trim

Trim

Continue with diagrams on page 16

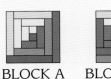

BLOCK A
Make 3
for each row

BLOCK B
Make 3
for each row

2a-b.

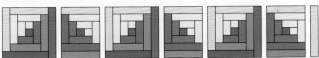

Add another sky strip

2c.

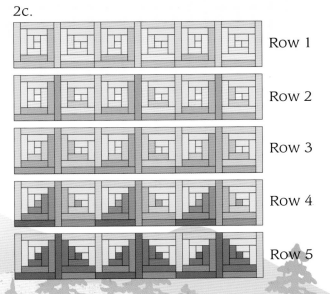

Row 1

Row 2

Row 3

Row 4

Row 5

30 x 30″

Use fabric with 42″ usable width.

When strips appear in cutting list, cut crossgrain strips (selvage to selvage) unless otherwise noted.

YARDAGE

Red-violet	leaf, Borders 1 & 3	⅝ yd
Brown	leaf	⅙ yd
Light brown	leaf background	⅙ yd
Green	frame	⅙ yd
Gray-blue	large triangles	⅓ yd
Rust	Border 1	⅛ yd
Medium brown	Border 1	⅛ yd
Gold	Border 2	⅙ yd
Light purple	Border 2	⅓ yd
Cream	Border 2	⅓ yd
Binding		⅜ yd
Backing		1⅛ yd
Batting		34 x 34″

CUTTING   *Cut in HALF diagonally

Red-violet	leaf	*2 squares 3⅞″
	Border 1	*8 squares 2⅜″
		8 squares 2″
	Border 3	4 strips 3½″ wide
Brown	leaf	3 squares 3½″
	stem	1 piece 1 x 6″
Light brown	leaf background	1 square 3½″
		*2 squares 3⅞″
	stem unit	*1 square 4″
Green	frame	2 pieces 1⅜ x 9½″
		2 pieces 1⅜ x 11⅛″
Gray-blue	large triangles	*2 squares 8⅜″
Rust	Border 1	4 pieces 2 x 9½″
Medium brown	Border 1	*8 squares 2⅜″
		4 squares 2″
Gold	Border 2	4 pieces 3½ x 6½″
Light purple	Border 2	*8 squares 3⅞″
		4 squares 3½″
Cream	Border 2	*8 squares 3⅞″
		8 squares 3½″
Binding		4 strips 2½″ wide

DIRECTIONS

Use ¼″ seam allowance unless otherwise noted.

1. LEAF BLOCK & FRAME: Make leaf block using directions and diagrams for Step 1 on page 12.

Press. Stitch short frame pieces to opposite sides. Stitch long frame pieces to remaining sides. Press.

2. LARGE SETTING TRIANGLES: Stitch large triangles to opposite sides. Stitch large triangles to remaining sides. Press.

3. BORDERS 1 & 2: Refer to directions and diagrams on pages 10-11 (Borders 2 and 3 of Cabin in the Woods quilt).

4. BORDER 3: Measure length of quilt. Cut border strips to this measurement and stitch to sides of quilt. Measure width of quilt. Cut border strips to this measurement for top and bottom of quilt. Stitch to quilt. Press.

5. LAYER, QUILT, & BIND: Cut backing to same size as batting. Layer, baste, and quilt as desired. Trim backing and batting even with top. Stitch binding strips together end to end. Press in half lengthwise, wrong sides together. Bind quilt using ⅜″ seam allowance.

1.

2.

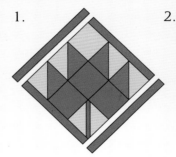

3.

3.

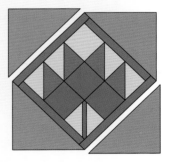

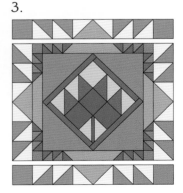

56x66"

Use fabric with 42" usable width.

When strips appear in cutting list, cut crossgrain strips (selvage to selvage) unless otherwise noted.

YARDAGE

Blues	Geese	⅛ yd ea of 13 or more fabrics
Creams	Geese	⅛ yd ea of 13 or more fabrics
Navy	sashing	⅔ yd
Cream	Border 1, setting strips	1¾ yd
Navy plaid	Border 2	1⅓ yd
Binding		⅝ yd
Backing		3¾ yd
Batting		62x72"

CUTTING

Blues	100 pieces 2½x4½"
Creams	200 squares 2½"
Sashing	13 strips 1½" wide
Border 1	4 strips 1½" wide (cut on lengthwise grain)
Setting strips	3 strips 6½" wide (cut on lengthwise grain)
Border 2	6 strips 6½" wide
Binding	7 strips 2½" wide

DIRECTIONS

Use ¼" seam allowance unless otherwise noted.

1. FLYING GEESE ROWS: Make 100 units following diagrams. Press. Stitch together into 4 vertical rows of 25 units. Press.

2. SASHING & SETTING STRIPS

   a. Measure length of Flying Geese rows. Piece 8 sashing strips this length and stitch one to each side of each Flying Geese row. Press.

   b. Cut 3 setting strips this measurement and stitch to Flying Geese rows, alternating, as shown.

   c. Measure width of quilt. Piece 2 sashing strips to this length and stitch to top and bottom of quilt. Press.

3. BORDER 1: Measure length of quilt. Cut border strips to this measurement and stitch to sides of quilt. Measure width of quilt. Cut border strips to this measurement for top and bottom of quilt. Stitch to quilt. Press.

4. BORDER 2: Repeat Step 3, piecing border strips where needed.

5. LAYER, QUILT, & BIND: Piece backing horizontally to same size as batting. Layer, baste, and quilt as desired. Trim backing and batting even with top. Stitch binding strips together end to end. Press in half lengthwise, wrong sides together. Bind quilt using ⅜" seam allowance.

1.

Stitch   Trim   Repeat   Make 100

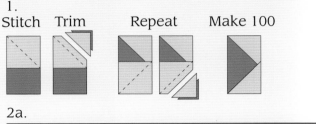

2a.

2b-c.

36x36″

Use fabric with 42″ usable width.

When strips appear in cutting list, cut crossgrain strips (selvage to selvage) unless otherwise noted.

Patterns, pages 42-43, are given for fusible web applique, reversed and ready to be traced. Be sure to have plenty of fusible web on hand if using this method. Reverse patterns and add seam allowance if doing hand applique.

YARDAGE

Blues	blocks	⅛ yd each of 9 fabrics
	Border 2	¼ yd
	Border 4	⅞ yd
	columbines	¼ yd
Yellows	blocks, Border 3, columbines	⅙ yd each of 5 fabrics
	Border 1	⅙ yd
Medium green	leaves, vines	⅓ yd
Light green	leaves	⅛ yd
White	columbines	⅛ yd
Binding		⅜ yd
Backing		1¼ yd
Batting		40x40″

CUTTING

Blues	blocks	1 strip 1½″ of each
	Border 2	2 strips 3″ wide
	Border 4	4 strips 6½″ wide
	columbines & tails	4 large, 8 small
Yellows	blocks	1 strip 1½″ of each
	Border 3	12 squares 2″ of each
	Border 1	2 strips 1½″ wide
	columbine centers	4 large, 8 small
Med green	leaves, vines	8 large, 4 vines of 3 segments each
Lt green	leaves	8 small
White	columbine centers	4 large, 8 small
Binding		4 strips 2½″ wide

Continued on page 41.

1. Make 4

2.

3.

4.

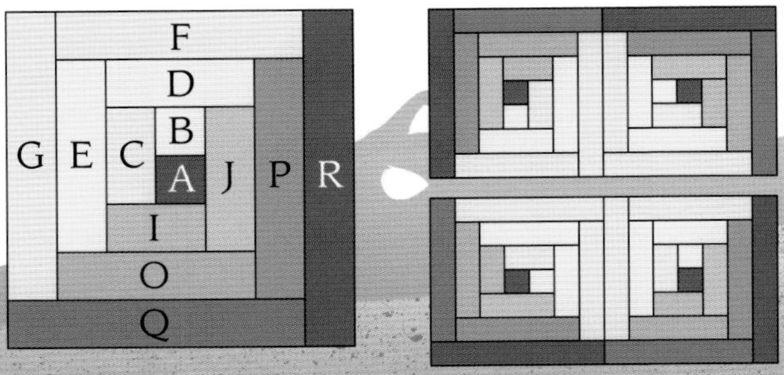

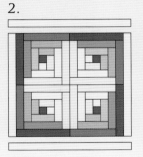

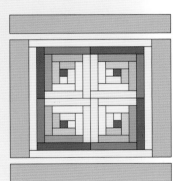

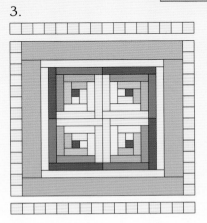

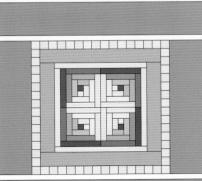

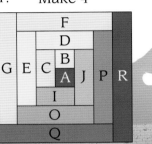

46 x 46″

Use fabric with 42″ usable width.

When strips appear in cutting list, cut crossgrain strips (selvage to selvage).

YARDAGE

White	1⅜ yd
Tan	⅛ yd
Greens #1, 2, 3, 4	¼ yd each
Purple, mauve	⅓ yd each
Lavender	¼ yd
Blues #1, 2, 4	⅝ yd each (#1 is darkest)
Blues #3, 5, 6	⅜ yd each (#6 is lightest)
Binding	½ yd
Backing	3¼ yd
Batting	52 x 52″

CUTTING   *Cut these squares in HALF diagonally

White	5th row tree	8 pieces 2½ x 4¾″
	Bdr 4 Flying Geese	48 pieces 2½ x 4½″
	Border 4 corners	*2 squares 4⅞″
	Border 3	4 pieces 2½ x 10½″
	Border 3	4 pieces 2½ x 12½″
	Border 5	4 pieces 2½ x 16½″
	Border 5	4 pieces 2½ x 18½″
Tan	tree trunks	4 pieces 2 x 2½″
Green #1	1st row tree	4 pieces 2½ x 4½″
Green #2	2nd row tree	4 pieces 2½ x 6½″
Green #3	3rd row tree	4 pieces 2½ x 8½″
	center	4 squares 3½″
Green #4	4th row tree	4 pieces 2½ x 10½″
Purple	center corners	4 squares 3½″
	center triangles	*8 squares 3⅞″
Lavender	center triangles	*4 squares 3⅞″
Mauve	center squares	6 squares 3½″
	center Flying Geese	4 pieces 3½ x 6½″
Blue #1	1st row sky	8 pieces 2½ x 5½″
	center triangles	*4 squares 3⅞″
	Border 1	2 pieces 1½ x 24½″
		2 pieces 1½ x 26½″
	Border 4 corners	*2 squares 4⅞″
Blue #2	2nd row sky	8 pieces 2½ x 4½″
	center triangles	*8 squares 3⅞″
	center Flying Geese	8 squares 3½″
Blue #3	3rd row sky	8 pieces 2½ x 3½″
	Border 2	4 pieces 2½ x 8½″
		4 pieces 2½ x 10½″
Blue #4	Bdr 4 Flying Geese	96 squares 2½″
Blue #5	center squares	6 squares 3½″
Blue #6	center squares	4 squares 3½″
	center triangles	*8 squares 3⅞″
	4th row sky	8 squares 2½″
Binding		5 strips 2¼″ wide

DIRECTIONS

Use ¼″ seam allowance unless otherwise noted.

1. CENTER BLOCK

   a. Make 8 half-square triangle units with lavender and blue #6. Make 8 with blue #1 and blue #6. Press.

   b. Make 2 quarter blocks with mauve and green #3 squares and lavender half-square triangle units. Make 2 with blue #5 and green #3 squares, and blue half-square triangle units. Press.

   c. Alternating and rotating quarter blocks as shown, stitch into block. Press.

   d. Make 16 purple and blue #2 half-square triangle units. Make 4 Flying Geese units with mauve rectangles and blue #2 squares, referring to directions and diagrams on page 15. Press.

   e. Stitch units from previous step and purple squares into 2 side borders and top and bottom borders as shown. Press. Stitch to block. Press.

Continued on page 40.

1a-b.

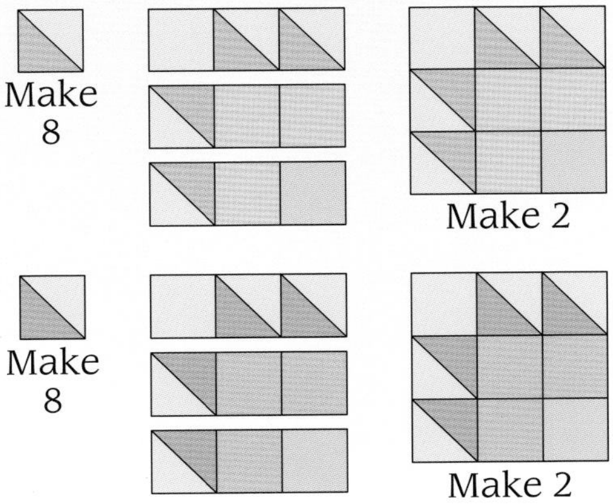

Make 8   Make 2

Make 8   Make 2

1c.

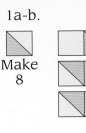

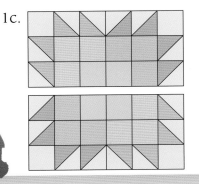

Frosty Morn

Continued from page 39.

2. BORDERS

   a. Make 48 Flying Geese units with white rectangles and blue #4 squares, referring to directions and diagrams on page 15. Press. Make 8 border units with 6 Flying Geese units each. Press.

   b. Make 4 half-square triangle units with white and blue #1 for Border 4 corners. Press.

   c. Make 4 each of the tree block rows, referring to directions and diagrams on page 13. Stitch row 2 and row 3 together. Do not stitch remaining rows together. Press.

   d. Prepare Side Borders: Make 2 of each. Stitch first row of tree block to shorter white Border 5 pieces. Stitch rows 2/3 of tree block to Flying Geese units as shown. Stitch fourth row of tree block to shorter white Border 3 pieces. Stitch fifth row of tree block to shorter Border 2 pieces. Press.

   e. Prepare Top and Bottom Borders: Make 2 of each. Stitch first row of tree block to longer white Border 5 pieces. Stitch rows 2/3 of tree block, Flying Geese units, and Border 4 corner units as shown. Stitch fourth row of tree block to longer white Border 3 pieces. Stitch fifth row of tree block to longer Border 2 pieces. Press.

   f. Stitch shorter Border 1 pieces to sides of quilt. Stitch longer Border 1 pieces to top and bottom. Press.

   g. For Border 2, stitch side border units on first, then top and bottom border units. Press. Repeat for Borders 3-5.

3. LAYER, QUILT, & BIND: Piece backing to same size as batting. Layer, baste, and quilt as desired. Trim backing and batting even with top. Stitch binding strips together end to end. Press in half lengthwise, wrong sides together. Bind quilt using ¼" seam allowance.

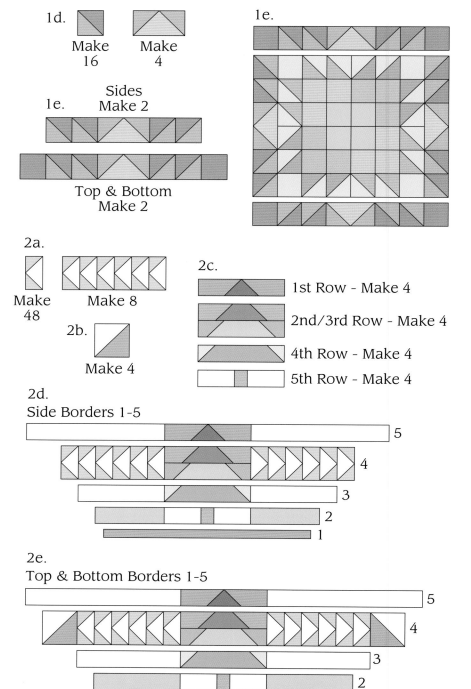

1d.
Make 16   Make 4

1e. Sides Make 2

1e. Top & Bottom Make 2

1e.

2a. Make 48   Make 8

2b. Make 4

2c.
1st Row - Make 4
2nd/3rd Row - Make 4
4th Row - Make 4
5th Row - Make 4

2d. Side Borders 1-5

2e. Top & Bottom Borders 1-5

2f. Border 1
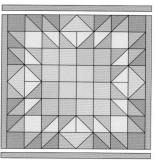

2f. Border 2
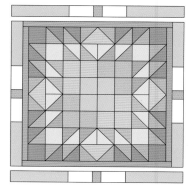

WREATH & CABIN WALL HANGINGS

Continued from page 23.

DIRECTIONS

Use ¼" seam allowance unless otherwise noted.

WREATH

1. BLOCK: Trace to fusible web 11 oak leaves, 4 large aspen leaves, 7 small aspen leaves, and 10 sets of acorn parts. Fuse to appropriate fabrics. Fuse appliques to background square using photo as a guide. Applique with desired machine stitch.

2. BORDER 1: Stitch shorter Border 1 pieces to sides of block. Stitch longer pieces to top and bottom. Press.

3. BORDER 2: Refer to Step 2 and diagrams on page 15. Mix fabrics as desired. Make 36 units and stitch into 4 borders of 9 units each. Press. Stitch one to each side of wall hanging. Stitch 4½" squares to each end of remaining borders. Stitch to top and bottom of wall hanging. Press.

4. LAYER, QUILT, & BIND: Cut backing to same size as batting. Layer, baste, and quilt as desired. Trim backing and batting even with top. Stitch binding strips together end to end. Press in half lengthwise, wrong sides together. Bind quilt using ¼" seam allowance.

CABIN

1. BLOCK: Make cabin block referring to directions on page 9 and using 1½" strips as desired to cut "logs" (pieces K-T).

2. BORDER 1: Stitch shorter Border 1 pieces to sides of block. Stitch longer pieces to top and bottom. Press.

3. BORDER 2: Repeat Step 2.

4. BORDER 3: Refer to Step 3 of Wreath directions above.

5. LAYER, QUILT, & BIND: Refer to Step 4 of Wreath directions above.

ROCKY MOUNTAIN COLUMBINE

Continued from page 37.

DIRECTIONS

Use ¼" seam allowance unless otherwise noted.

1. BLOCKS: Follow directions in Steps 1-2 on page 16. Mixing fabrics as desired, cut 4 each of B-G from assorted yellows, and 4 each of A, I, J, O-R from assorted blues. See diagrams on page 37 and 16. Make 4 blocks. Press. Stitch blocks into 2 rows as shown. Stitch rows together. Press.

2. BORDERS 1 & 2: Measure length of quilt. Cut border strips to this measurement and stitch to sides of quilt. Measure width of quilt. Cut border strips to this measurement for top and bottom of quilt. Stitch to quilt. Press.

3. BORDER 3: Stitch squares into 2 borders of 14 squares and 2 borders of 16 squares. Press. Stitch short borders to sides. Stitch long borders to top and bottom. Press.

4. BORDER 4: Repeat Step 2.

5. APPLIQUE: Applique Border 4 using photo as a guide. See Spring & Fall Borders, page 17, for specific vine directions. Cut fusible web for vine 3 x 20".

6. LAYER, QUILT, & BIND: Cut backing to same size as batting. Layer, baste, and quilt as desired. Trim backing and batting even with top. Stitch binding strips together end to end. Press in half lengthwise, wrong sides together. Bind quilt using ⅜" seam allowance.

Experiment with the blocks to make your own creations like this table runner.

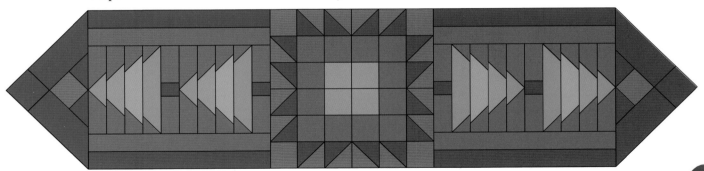

CABIN
IN THE WOODS

ROCKY
MOUNTAIN
COLUMBINES

Patterns are for fusible web applique, reversed for tracing and no seam allowance added.

CABIN IN THE WOODS

AUTUMN LEAVES

Stem Unit for Leaf Block

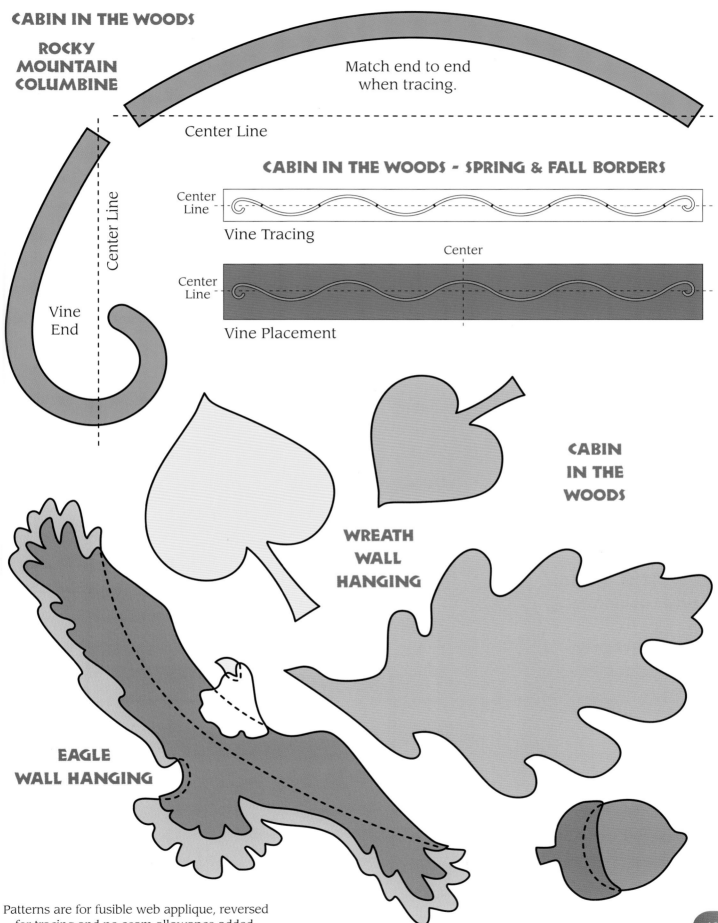

CABIN IN THE WOODS

ROCKY MOUNTAIN COLUMBINE

Match end to end when tracing.

Center Line

Center Line

Vine End

CABIN IN THE WOODS – SPRING & FALL BORDERS

Center Line

Vine Tracing

Center

Center Line

Vine Placement

CABIN IN THE WOODS

WREATH WALL HANGING

EAGLE WALL HANGING

Patterns are for fusible web applique, reversed for tracing and no seam allowance added.

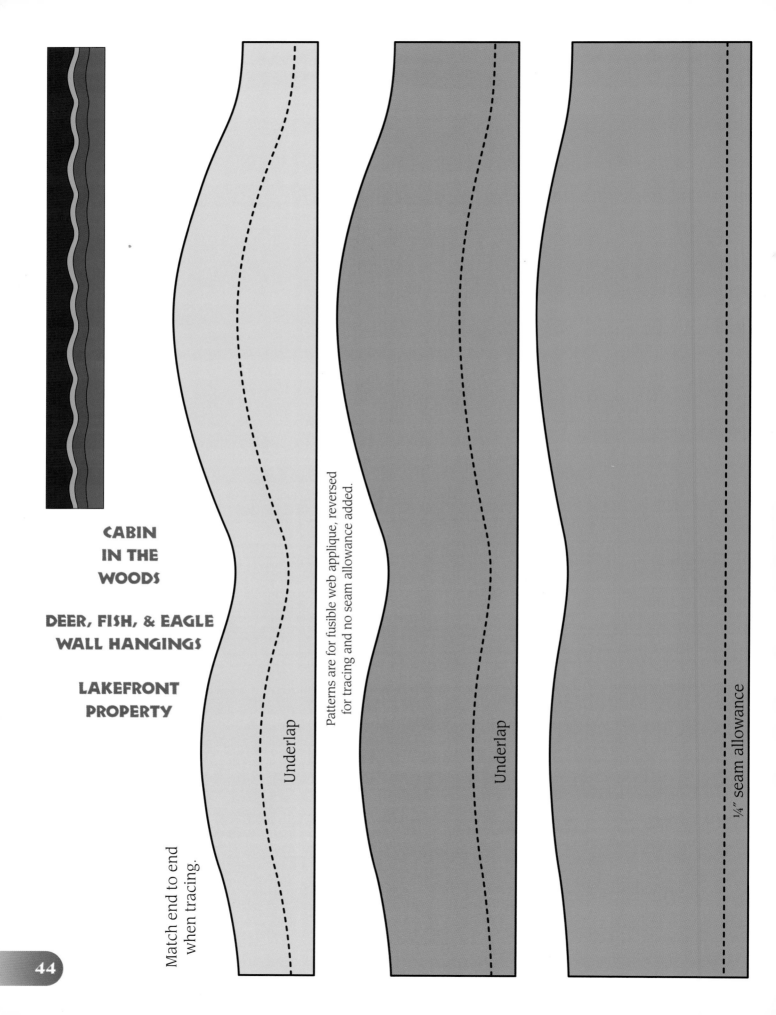

CABIN IN THE WOODS

DEER, FISH, & EAGLE WALL HANGINGS

LAKEFRONT PROPERTY

Match end to end when tracing.

Underlap

Patterns are for fusible web applique, reversed for tracing and no seam allowance added.

Underlap

¼" seam allowance

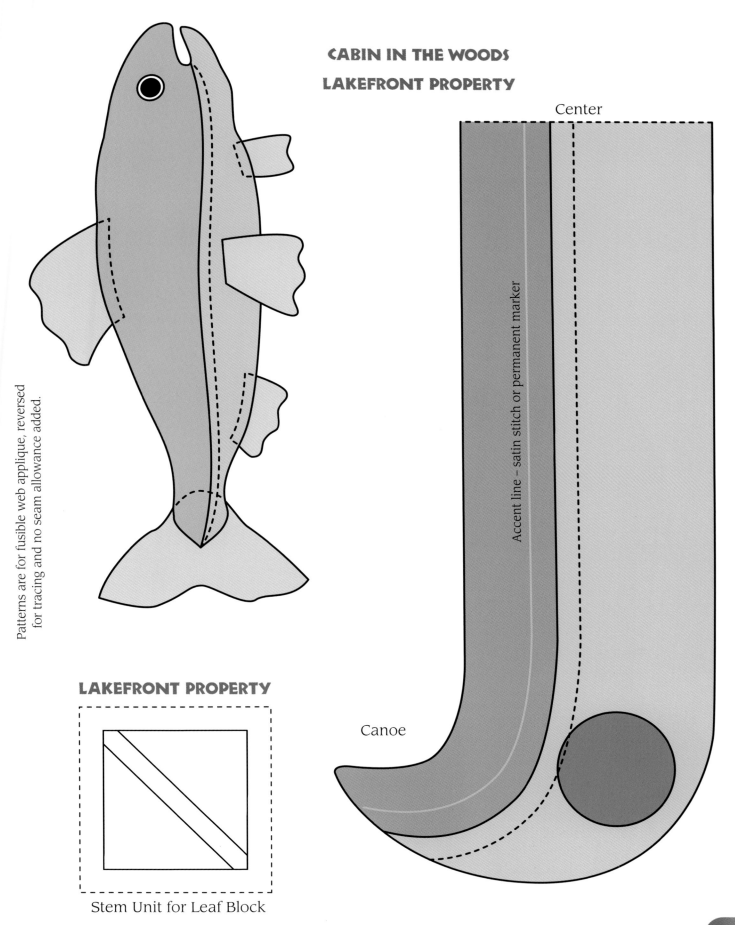

Patterns are for fusible web applique, reversed for tracing and no seam allowance added.

CABIN IN THE WOODS
LAKEFRONT PROPERTY

Center

Accent line – satin stitch or permanent marker

Canoe

LAKEFRONT PROPERTY

Stem Unit for Leaf Block

CABIN IN THE WOODS
MOUNTAIN CROSSING

Patterns are for fusible web applique, reversed for tracing and no seam allowance added.

Match to dotted line at right

Match to dotted line at left

CABIN IN THE WOODS

DEER WALL HANGING

Patterns are for fusible web applique, reversed for tracing and no seam allowance added.

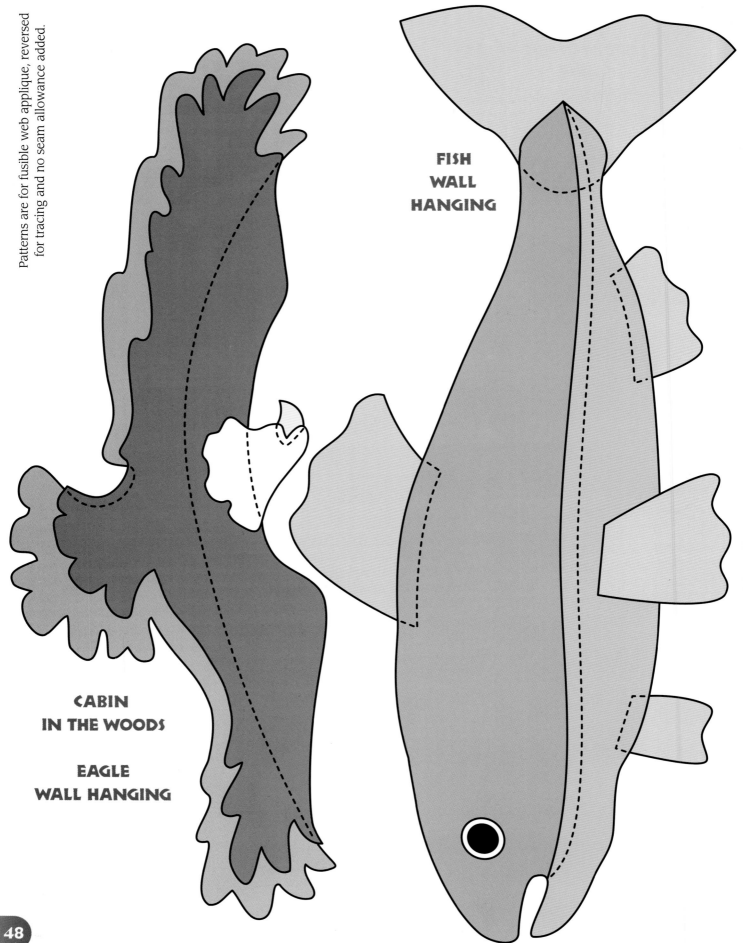

Patterns are for fusible web applique, reversed for tracing and no seam allowance added.

FISH WALL HANGING

CABIN IN THE WOODS

EAGLE WALL HANGING

48